The First Twenty-One

Tahia Towhidul

BookLeaf Publishing

India | USA | UK

Presentation by *BookLeaf Publishing*

Web: www.bookleafpub.com

E-mail: info@bookleafpub.com

ISBN: 9789357214865

First edition 2022

*No matter what, I love my Ammu and Baba
and I thank them for everything they have
done for me. And to my friends and my little
sister, you already know.*

PREFACE

Growing up I felt a lot of emotions - I felt really, really sad, insecure about myself, confused about who I am, and even in love. When I felt these feelings so deeply, I turned to poetry. I turned to words to see if I can make sense of what I was feeling or at the very least get those feelings out of my system. For the most part, it worked. Those poems I have written over the twenty-one years of my life have been collated and have been given to you and maybe you can empathise to what I've felt too.

Growing Down

It's funny how you don't notice,
You don't think there's anything wrong
With you, about you
Until you want to be desired.
Suddenly your world comes crashing
Down, every comment bearing more and more
weight-
Then suddenly you're
Stuck.
All because you grew up.

Feeling Left Out

2

I like the way that I am. Who I am.
A fiery goddess, full of energy and life.
I see everything in a good light
And express my love for the universe and people
In any way that I can.
Others; not so much.
To them
I am intense
Annoying
Weird
A bit too much for a young lady.
I try not to care because I know who I am
And I love her.
But I also love the people of this world...
Why can't they love me back?

Being Unique

I worry
Lay awake
Considering whether or not
I really am anything.
Am I funny, kind, witty, confident.
Do I have a personality?
I throw myself into hobbies
Create a roster
Ukulele, crochet, poetry
Anything so that I am not just a name.
Besides on the outside
I may not turn heads
And I may not naturally shine,
But if I can teach myself how to hot wire the
lights,
I can move them towards me
And show you my stories.
Then you'll realise I was always like them.
Hopefully, it's enough.

Thicker Than

Does blood run thicker than water?
I want to believe it does,
I've been raised as such.
Yet, I've seen what blind belief can do to you,
The way it broke my father.
The blood that was meant to preserve him
Yet he was there bleeding out.
He was stuck in the viscosity,
Between who he was and who he wanted to be.
How much pain does one endure
Because of the sharing of blood?
It's in our culture, it's what we've been told to do.
Yet I would not tolerate this from the people I
choose.
I shouldn't accept a pummelling
That breaks down my core
Because you're my family.

Choosing a Happiness

5

My happiness is important to me.
But so is theirs.
The issue is
Sometimes I have to pick.
Only one person gets to be happy-
It's a choice of who I love more:
Them or Me?

A Tan

I feared the sun for too long.
I was scared of its touch.
Worried that its grace would lessen mine.

They told me
"Don't stay outside too much, you'll tan! You
don't want to tan!"

Why don't I?
Of course I do.
I want my skin to reflect
My adventures
My bravery
My acceptance.

Now I run into the sun
Embracing its warmth
As I love myself.

The darkness of my skin does not devalue my
worth.

Moving Out

It's all in front of me now
Neatly laid
Organised
To how it should be.
Done by my mother who
Frankly sees more than I ever will.
She's packed piles of fabric in front of me.
What they really are, I do not know.
Perhaps a pillowcase, probably a duvet cover.

There's a box at my feet.
Sealed.
It seems that whatever is inside is all I need.
My mother says I'll always be prepared.
I wonderwhat's in there.

Soon, she won't do this packing anymore,
It'll just be me, these piles and boxes.
And I'm meant to know exactly
What I need for when
Since my life is all in front of me now.

Staying

I can't fathom the idea of a relationship
Particularly in my life.
It seems so unreachable
That someone would want to stay.

Daydream Scene

9

Today I walked into a room
And you didn't immediately catch my eye
But once I saw you
I was mesmerised.
You looked like a daydream scene
From a romance in the past.
The way your body was gracefully splayed
Your hands holding that book.
Instantly
I wanted to touch you, to join you
To become the daydream.
You were beautiful and I wanted you,
Oh, how I want you!

Weakness

Weakness
Is what I feel when I look at you
I go numb
I lose control
All because I looked at that face.

Perhaps I Am a Gymnast

On the outside, I am not the sporty type.
I'd much rather be at home,
On the sofa, with a film.
On the inside it seems to be a different narrative.
My stomach
Does flips and kicks.
A whole floor routine.
You see, my stomach is a gold medallist.
Its motivation is you.

Slow Burn

I long for the slow burn.
Each
Individual
Flame
Making its mark on my skin
Being careful not to mix.
The heat
Building
Collecting
Coursing through my veins.
Every day the steady warmth
Fuels my being.
The pain of the burn is worth the joy I feel.

The Best Bad Idea

Every neurone in my brain
Fired at once
Trying to stop me.
When considering what could happen, you were
a bad idea.

I ignored my brain
And went with the push of my heart
Telling me to take that leap.
I could feel all the happiness
That you had the potential to provide.

Neither my brain or my heart won.
Common sense gloats
As he leaves me to cry.
Emotion boasts
Every time he makes me smile.

You are the best bad idea I could've had.

Action Potential

Every time you touch me,
Sparks rush violently through my body.
So much action going on you can't see,
Just at the potential of what we could be.

Detailing

15

I have this urge to tell you everything.
I want to share every aspect of my life with you.
I want you to know where I am,
Where I'll be,
Who I'm with.
And I want every detail in return.

Selective Listening

I am listening.
Just not to your speaking.
I listen to the way
Your blue eyes sparkle
When something finally makes sense.
I listen to the way your curls bounce, poised,
After you so delicately placed them there.
I listen to the way your knuckles click
As you focus with content.
I lsiten to the way your heartbeat races
As I lie my head on your chest.
So yes, I did laugh at your joke five minutes
late.
But I was too busy listening to all of you,
Your dad joke could wait.

You Like My Crazy

I can't think straight,
I never do.
Every thought I have is convoluted,
Messy, up, left, down, back,
Organised chaos.
For me, there are never straight paths through a
woods;
I admire the nature as it blooms spontaneously
around me
Inspect the green of the oak tree, collect the
acorns below,
Take pride in the crunch of the snow in the
untouched corner.
It's been hard for anyone else to follow
Let alone enjoy. But you
You carry around sweet breadcrumbs
You don't get lost
You go up into the mud with me and
Left then down to the sky.
You love me so much that you don't go back
And we revel in the organised chaos.

Burnt By Lava

I had to say goodbye.
We couldn't keep going at the rate we were
going.
You kept me warm and I loved it.
I closed my eyes and I basked in you.
I just didn't realise I was drowning
In this lava,
Being consumed
Burning.
It was the hardest feat I faced,
Climbing, crawling, crying out.
I saved myself- but now
I'm cold.

The Risk

I took a risk.
A really big one.
If it had paid off- I would've been
On top of the world. A winner in every way.
Except it didn't.
I landed with a thud and plenty of broken bones
And now I can't walk the same,
Feel the same, love the same.
Everything has changed; but for the worst.
I miss it all.
I miss you.

Cried In The Shower

I've been getting up,
Brushing my teeth and
Living these days.
These days without you
I've been keeping on going,
Moving on and
Smiling through time.
But today
I cried in the shower
Because suddenly I remembered it all;
How it's so different now.
But then my day continued.
As did yours.

Thinking About You At 2am

21

Those times
When I lay awake
Trying
Forcing
To have another thought
I always end with a question.
I wonder whether you think about me
As much as I think about you
The way that I do.